# The World of Perception

'In simple prose Merleau-Ponty touches on his principal themes. He speaks about the body and the
world, the coexistence of space and things, the
unfortunate optimism of science – and also the
insidious stickiness of honey, and the mystery of
anger.'

*James Elkins*, Author of *Stories of Art*

'Merleau-Ponty is one of the seminal thinkers of the
post-war period, and these short talks to a radio
audience, from a relatively early moment in his writing career, show his humane intelligence at work.'

*Michael Fried, Johns Hopkins University*

Routledge Classics contains the very best of Routledge publishing over the past century or so, books that have, by popular consent, become established as classics in their field. Drawing on a fantastic heritage of innovative writing published by Routledge and its associated imprints, this series makes available in attractive, affordable form some of the most important works of modern times.

For a complete list of titles visit
www.routledge.com/classics

Maurice
# Merleau-Ponty

## The World of Perception

Translated by Oliver Davis

With a foreword by Stéphanie Ménasé
and an introduction by Thomas Baldwin

 London and New York

First published in French as *Causeries 1948*
© Editions de Seuil, 2002

This translation first published 2004
by Routledge

First published in Routledge Classics 2008
by Routledge
2 Park Square, Milton Park, Abingdon, Oxon OX14 4RN

Simultaneously published in the USA and Canada
by Routledge
711 Third Ave, New York, NY 10017

*Routledge is an imprint of the Taylor & Francis Group, an informa business*

Translation © Routledge 2004

Introduction © Thomas Baldwin 2004

Typeset in Joanna by RefineCatch Limited, Bungay, Suffolk
Printed and bound by CPI Group (UK) Ltd, Croydon, CR0 4YY

*British Library Cataloguing in Publication Data*
A catalogue record for this book is available from the British Library

*Library of Congress Cataloging in Publication Data*
A catalog record for this book has been requested

ISBN10: 0–415–77381–4
ISBN13: 978–0–415–77381–2

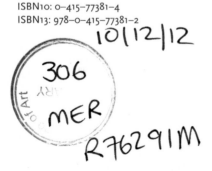

# CONTENTS

# FOREWORD

The seven lectures collected in this volume were commissioned by French national radio and broadcast on its National Programme at the end of 1948. Copies have been kept at the Institut National de l'Audiovisuel for use by researchers and other professionals alike.

These seven talks were written by Maurice Merleau-Ponty for a series of radio broadcasts and delivered by him in 1948.[1] According to the official radio listings, six were broadcast on the French national station, one each week, between Saturday 9 October and Saturday 13 November 1948. The lectures were recorded for a programme called 'The French Culture Hour' and were read continuously, without interruption. Copies of the recordings have been kept at the Institut National de l'Audiovisuel (INA).

On Saturdays, the general theme of this programme was 'The development of ideas'. Merleau-Ponty's lectures were broadcast on the same day as others by Georges Davy (on the psychology of primitive peoples), Emmanuel Mounier (on the psychology of character), Maxime Laignel-Lavastine (on psychoanalysis) and Emile Henriot of the Académie Française (on psychological themes in literature). The INA's archives suggest that there is no surviving record of the preamble introducing the speakers and specifying the precise topic of each broadcast.

The lectures were devised by Merleau-Ponty to form a series and it was he who decided on their order and individual titles: (1) The World of Perception and the World of Science; (2) Exploring the World of Perception: Space; (3) Exploring the World of Perception: Sensory Objects; (4) Exploring the World of Perception: Animal Life; (5) Man Seen from the Outside; (6) Art and the World of Perception; (7) Classical World, Modern World.

This edition is based on the typewritten text prepared by Merleau-Ponty from his written plan. These papers (which are part of a private collection) carry corrections in the author's own hand.

The recording is, for the most part, a faithful rendition by Merleau-Ponty of his written text. Bibliographical references are preceded by a number. We have endeavoured to go back to the editions available to Merleau-Ponty and his contemporaries. Our research reveals just how scrupulously attentive Merleau-Ponty was to recent and newly published work. Books referred to are listed in the bibliography at the end of the volume.

We would like to express our particular thanks to those at the INA who have assisted us in our research into the broadcasting of these lectures.

*Stéphanie Ménasé*

# INTRODUCTION

## Thomas Baldwin

### MAURICE MERLEAU-PONTY (1908–61)

Merleau-Ponty was one of the most creative philosophers of the twentieth century. He combined a new way of thinking about the basic structures of human life with reflections on art, literature and politics which draw on this new philosophy. These lively radio talks from 1948 show him at the height of his powers, moving easily between philosophical themes and discussions of painting and politics; the emphasis on painting is indeed specially notable here, as is the way in which he uses this to indicate his philosophical themes. The result is a brief text which provides the best possible introduction to his philosophy, especially since this is dominated by a larger and more complex text published in 1945 – *Phenomenology of Perception*.[1] But these talks should also be valued in their own right, for in many respects the contrasts with the past which Merleau-Ponty draws and the anxieties which he articulates are still ours. In my own introduction, after a brief account of Merleau-Ponty's life and philosophy, I shall say a little about each talk ('lecture'), connecting them with Merleau-Ponty's other writings, and also reflecting briefly on their significance for us.

## LIFE

Merleau-Ponty's father died in 1913 while he was still a small child, and, along with his brother and sister, he was brought up in Paris by his widowed mother. This situation of growing up without a father was one which he shared with Jean-Paul Sartre and Albert Camus, and was indeed common throughout Europe after the First World War.[2] In Merleau-Ponty's case, despite the absence of a father, this period seems to have been one of exceptional happiness and intimacy, and he carried the memory of it throughout his life:

> It is at the present time that I realize that the first twenty-five years of my life were a prolonged childhood, destined to be followed by a painful break leading eventually to independence. If I take myself back to those years as I actually lived them and as I carry them within me, my happiness at that time cannot be explained in terms of the sheltered atmosphere of the parental home; the

During the German occupation of France Merleau-Ponty initially joined Sartre, with whom he now became a close friend, in a quixotic attempt during 1941 to constitute an intellectual resistance movement ('Socialism and Freedom') distinct from the forces of the communists and the Gaullists.[6] This movement collapsed at the end of the year, largely because of its ineffectiveness; and Merleau-Ponty and Sartre then withdrew to write their major works of philosophy (Sartre's *Being and Nothingness* dates from this period).[7] Later in the war Sartre and Merleau-Ponty joined Camus in the group which published the resistance paper *Combat*, though they took little active part in the resistance. Nonetheless, the experience of the German occupation forced Merleau-Ponty to think much harder about politics than he had previously done,[8] and at the end of 1944 Merleau-Ponty was one of the group of leading intellectuals, led by Sartre and also including de Beauvoir and Aron, who founded the influential political journal *Les Temps Modernes*. Merleau-Ponty then helped Sartre edit the journal until 1950 when their different political judgments about communism made continued collaboration impossible.[9]

After the publication of *Phenomenology of Perception* in 1945 Merleau-Ponty's academic career progressed quickly. In 1945 he was appointed a Professor at Lyon; in 1950 he became Professor of Psychology at the Sorbonne in Paris; and then in 1952 he was appointed to the most prestigious position for a French philosopher, the chair in philosophy at the Collège de France, a position which he held until his unexpected early death in 1961. During this period he published three collections of essays: *Sense and Non-Sense* (1948) which brings together his early post-1945 essays, of which most are about Marxism and politics;[10] *The Adventures of the Dialectic* (1955) which deals with his break with Sartre and includes his later thoughts about 'Western' Marxism;[11] finally, *Signs* (1960) which contains some new philosophical work, mainly on language, together with further political essays.[12] After his death it became apparent that Merleau-Ponty had been working on a major new monograph. This had originally been intended as a study of language and truth which would develop themes from the earlier writings under the title 'The Origin of Truth'; but as the work progressed Merleau-Ponty found himself drawn back to some of the themes concerning perception that he had addressed in his earlier philosophy, and the manuscript that was published posthumously in 1964 bears Merleau-Ponty's later working title, *The Visible and the Invisible*.[13]

After his death Merleau-Ponty's reputation in France declined quickly as French philosophers turned away from French existential phenomenology to the study of German philosophy, especially to the works of Heidegger and the 'masters of suspicion' – Marx, Nietzsche and Freud. Elsewhere, however, and especially in the United States, his former pupils preserved his reputation and ensured the translation into English of all his major works. More recently, within the analytic tradition, there has been a growth of interest in his writings: his discussions of the 'intentionality' of consciousness (especially of the ways in which things are presented in perception) and of the role of the body in perception are recognised as important contributions to the understanding of these difficult topics. It is to be hoped that these radio talks will help to make his ideas available to a wider public here, just as their publication in France in 2002 is evidence of a long overdue revival of interest there in his work.

## MERLEAU-PONTY'S PHILOSOPHY: PERCEPTION AND THE BODY

Merleau-Ponty sets out his main aim for these lectures at the end of the first paragraph of this first lecture: 'I shall suggest . . . that one of the great achievements of modern art and philosophy . . . has been to allow us to rediscover the world in which we live, yet which we are always prone to forget'. This world which we are to rediscover is the 'world of perception', which is the world *as* we perceive it, the 'perceived world' (*le monde perçu*) as it is often called. Merleau-Ponty devotes most of his lectures to explorations of this perceived world, in order to enable his audience to 'rediscover' it for themselves. But he does not explain straightforwardly why this rediscovery is so important. Since this point is a central theme of *Phenomenology of Perception* it is worth saying a little about it here in order to help readers of these lectures understand where Merleau-Ponty is coming from.

Any philosophy which seeks to take us back to the perceived world is, in its general perspective, empiricist; and Merleau-Ponty signals his empiricism when he explicitly endorses Berkeley's thesis that 'we cannot conceive anything that is not perceived or perceptible'.[14] The classical empiricism of Berkeley and Hume, however, is based on the claim that the contents of thought are restricted to possible contents of sense experience, and this thesis was famously revived by the Logical Positivist philosophers of the 1930s when they affirmed the 'verification principle' that the meaning of a proposition is given by its method of verification, i.e. by the way in which its truth or falsity can be settled on the basis of observation. Merleau-Ponty makes it clear, however, that his empiricism is not of this kind. This is partly because he rejects the emphasis on 'scientific' observation that was characteristic of the logical positivists; this connects with the critical attitude to the status of science he adopts in the first lecture, which I discuss below. But, more fundamentally, Merleau-Ponty follows Husserl in taking it that the relationship between perception and all other modes of thought, including science, is one of 'Fundierung' (foundation), which involves a kind of rootedness that does not restrict the capacity for more sophisticated articulations of experience in the light of deeper understandings of the world. So he consistently rejects those forms of empiricism which aim to restrict or reduce the contents of thought to possible contents of experience.[15]

A further respect in which Merleau-Ponty departs from classical empiricism concerns the 'a priori'. Classical empiricists held that because all our ideas are derived from experience, there is no legitimate role for ideas, or concepts, which are not thus derived, even where there is no obvious account of such a derivation, as with mathematical concepts such as infinity. The 'rationalist' philosophers, as opposed to the empiricists, such as Descartes (whom Merleau-Ponty uses as a foil throughout these lectures), held that ideas are innate within the mind, and that the role of experience was primarily just to bring them into use by us.

-----

This hypothesis was not easy to believe, but Kant famously moved the debate forward by distinguishing between a priori concepts, such as identity, that are integral to the possibility of experience and thought, and empirical concepts that are acquired on the basis of experience and are answerable to the ways of thinking about the world which are best confirmed by experience. Thus Kant held that while the empiricists were largely right about empirical concepts, the rationalists were largely right about a priori concepts, which are the most important ones for philosophy. Most subsequent philosophers have agreed with Kant on this point, and Merleau-Ponty certainly does. But he gives a very distinctive twist to the Kantian position, by maintaining that our embodiment is integral to the role of a priori concepts in sense experience. He sets out his attitude to Kant in the following passage:

> Kant saw clearly that the problem is not how determinate shapes and sizes make their appearance in my experience, since without them there would be no experience, and since any internal experience is possible only against the background of external experience. But Kant's conclusion from this was that I am a consciousness which embraces and constitutes the world, and this reflection caused him to overlook the phenomenon of the body and that of the thing.[16]

The central theme of Merleau-Ponty's philosophy, from *The Structure of Behavior* to *The Visible and the Invisible*, is precisely the way in which 'the phenomenon of the body' is to be integrated into a Kantian philosophy, so that each of us is not so much a 'consciousness' as a body which 'embraces and constitutes the world'. He puts the point in *Phenomenology of Perception* in the following way: 'by thus remaking contact with the body and with the world, we shall rediscover ourself, since, perceiving as we do with our body, the body is a natural self and, as it were, the subject of perception.'[17] His main claim is, then, that our embodiment brings to our perceptual experience an a priori structure whereby it presents itself to us in consciousness as experience of a world of things in space and time whose nature is independent of us. It is our 'bodily' intentionality which brings the possibility of meaning into our experience by ensuring that its content, the things presented in experience, are surrounded with references to the past and future, to other places and other things, to human possibilities and situations.

This sounds like a psychological thesis; and indeed it is one, substantiated by Merleau-Ponty with detailed discussions from the psychological literature (mainly from the work of German psychologists of the 1930s, such as Kurt Goldstein). This very fact, however, invites the accusation of 'psychologism', of misrepresenting a psychological theory concerning the bodily contribution to the organisation of perception as a philosophical theory about the a priori structure of experience. Since Husserl's phenomenological method was precisely motivated by a wish to set himself apart from the 'psychologism', as he saw it, of his contemporaries, it would be ironic if Merleau-Ponty's phenomenology turned out to be a form of psychologism after all. But Merleau-Ponty anticipated this objection: his reply to it is that the alternatives 'psychological' and 'philosophical' are not exclusive. Precisely because man is 'transcendental', in the sense that man is the being which gives meaning to things, the 'psychological' understanding of man is at the same time a 'philosophical' understanding of the meaning of things. The accusation of 'psychologism' tacitly assumes that human psychology is a natural science, a branch of biology, whose ontology and methodology are to be thought of as comparable to other natural sciences. But Merleau-Ponty rejects this assumption: as he famously puts it in *Phenomenology of Perception*, perception is not a fact within the world, since it is the 'flaw' in this 'great diamond', the world;[18] because perception is the capacity whereby there is a world it cannot be just another fact within the world.

This line of thought can be questioned. It is not as clear as Merleau-Ponty assumes it to be that one cannot combine a conception of human perception as a natural fact with an acknowledgement of its special status as the root of the human understanding of the world. But this is not the place to take the argument further. Instead I want to return to the starting point of this discussion, to Merleau-Ponty's suggestion at the start of these lectures that we need to 'rediscover' the perceived world with the help of modern art and philosophy. On the face of it, as Merleau-Ponty acknowledges, this is an odd suggestion, since, surely, we are aware of the perceived world all the time that we are awake. But we can now begin to see why, for Merleau-Ponty, the 'natural attitude' of common sense leads us to overlook the phenomenon of the perceived world. For Merleau-Ponty's account of the role of the senses in perception is that they make it their business to cover their tracks as they organise experience in such a way that it presents to us a world of things arrayed before us in a three-dimensional objective space within which we are located as just another object. So as we get on with our life we do not notice the role of the senses in organising experience and 'constituting' the physical world; it is precisely their business to make this role invisible to us. Hence to rediscover and articulate it, we have somehow to get a detached, 'sideways', look at ordinary experience, and this is what, for Merleau-Ponty, modern art and phenomenological philosophy make possible. He characterised this kind of philosophical reflection in a memorable passage in the Preface to *Phenomenology of Perception*:

> Reflection does not withdraw from the world towards the unity of consciousness as the world's basis; it steps back to watch the forms of transcendence fly up like sparks from a fire; it slackens the intentional threads which attach us to the world and thus brings them to our notice; it alone is consciousness of the world because it reveals that world as strange and paradoxical.[19]

In these lectures, as we shall see, he complements this account of philosophy with a discussion of modern art in which he suggests that painters such as Cézanne likewise aim to make apparent to us the ways in which the emergence of the ordinary world in visual experience is 'strange and paradoxical'.

# MERLEAU-PONTY'S LECTURES

## Lecture 1: The world of perception and the world of science

As I have indicated, Merleau-Ponty opens his lectures by announcing that we need to rediscover the perceived world. I have tried to elucidate this demand by setting the lectures in the context of Merleau-Ponty's general philosophical project; and this will also help to elucidate the main thesis of the first lecture, which is that it would be quite wrong to suppose that the world of perception can be dismissed as mere 'appearance' in contrast with the 'real' world revealed by the natural sciences.

Merleau-Ponty describes the temptation to make this supposition as one which is 'particularly strong in France'. To a contemporary British reader this will seem an odd claim, since for us France is the land of the modern movements in art and literature, as well as of the postmodernism which denies any special status to the natural sciences. But it is good to be reminded that within France there has also been, as there still is, a strong tradition that takes the natural sciences as the paradigms of knowledge; and, as Merleau-Ponty indicates, this is a tradition that can be traced back to Descartes. Descartes took an extreme view of the unreliability of the senses; but a more common view would still be that the natural sciences show us that our ordinary perceptions of things are a poor guide to their fundamental structure. This is obvious if one thinks of, say, the molecular structure of physical substances, since this is invisible; but what is more striking is the way in which scientific enquiries can lead us to reorganise the classification of familiar objects, such that, for example, we come to take the view that whales are not fish.

Merleau-Ponty makes it clear that he does not contest the value of scientific inquiry. What he does reject is the thought that science penetrates 'to the heart of things, to the object as it is in itself'. Instead, he holds, science provides only abstract representations of aspects of the world that are of technological value, but which do not constitute 'absolute and complete knowledge'. It seems to me that Merleau-Ponty runs together different points here, in the closing paragraphs of his lecture. The thesis that the natural sciences might provide 'absolute and complete knowledge' of the world is an extreme view since there are many activities and interests, – sport, for example – such that facts about them are not, on the face of it, accessible to the natural sciences. To bring them within the compass of the natural sciences would require the hypothesis that the thoughts and movements of all those engaged in sport can somehow be brought within the compass of a scientific psychology that can be integrated into natural science. No great degree of scepticism is required to dismiss this hypothesis. But this gives too easy a triumph to the critic of science, since this kind of aspiration for absolute and complete knowledge is not essential to scientific inquiry. What is important is 'scientific realism', the belief that the account of the structure of things and forces provided by physics and other sciences does indeed reveal to us things that are really there, even if we cannot observe them, and the further belief that reference to this structure is of fundamental importance when we seek to explain natural phenomena.

When Merleau-Ponty says that science offers us only 'approximate expressions' of physical events, it is not clear whether he would reject scientific realism thus understood. For the scientific realist will of course allow that the accounts of structure provided by a science typically involve many approximations and simplifications, especially since the details needed vary from context to context (e.g. sometimes it is important to distinguish between the different isotopes of a molecule, sometimes not). The general implication of Merleau-Ponty's discussion, however, is undoubtedly hostile to scientific realism since, in effect, he seeks to reverse the application of the appearance/reality distinction to the relationship between the perceived world and the world of science. Unlike Descartes he holds that the perceived world is the 'real' world, as compared with which the world of science is just an approximation, i.e. an appearance. It seems to me, however, that these alternatives are not exhaustive. One does better to combine scientific realism with an acknowledgement that natural science is far from complete, and thus that there are important aspects of reality which escape science, including those which are manifest within the perceived world. These latter aspects are likely to be of fundamental importance for our primary understanding of things, just as those which are characteristic of the world of science are of fundamental importance when we seek to explain natural phenomena. There can also be different priorities here, and it is simply not necessary to take sides in the way that Merleau-Ponty appears to in order to defend the importance of an inquiry into the structure of the perceived world.

## Lecture 2: Exploring the world of perception: Space

Merleau-Ponty begins his 'exploration' of the perceived world with a discussion of space, and his basic theme is a contrast between the 'classical' conception of space and that which actually informs the world as we perceive it. The classical conception of space is that of Newtonian physics, which relies on a conception of 'absolute' space within which physical objects have an absolute location at a time and can move about without any alteration of their intrinsic physical properties.[20] Merleau-Ponty associates this conception of space with that found in 'classical' art, the kind of painting whereby objects are depicted in accordance with the perspective they would present when viewed under a gaze directed at a point of the horizon, what Merleau-Ponty calls 'a gaze fixed at infinity'. Such paintings, Merleau-Ponty says, 'remain at a distance and do not involve the viewer'; Merleau-Ponty gives no examples but one can perhaps think here of the paintings of the early Florentine Renaissance, or, in a French context, of the works of Nicholas Poussin.

Merleau-Ponty holds that this conception of space is misleading. In this context he is happy to begin by recruiting natural science to suggest that this conception of space does not even apply to the physical world. Merleau-Ponty is broadly right about this, though he gets the details wrong. It is not, as he suggests, the adoption of a non-Euclidean geometry that marks the downfall of the Newtonian conception of space, but the adoption by Einstein (in his general theory of relativity) of the nineteenth-century Riemann-Clifford hypothesis that geometry and physics are interdependent, in that gravity just expresses the curvature of space which is determined by the local distribution of matter. But Merleau-Ponty gives most attention to painting, and in particular to the manner in which Cézanne attempts to capture the way in which visual experience, through the distribution of colour, gives birth to the outline and shape of objects. Merleau-Ponty notes that in doing this Cézanne breaks with the traditional laws of perspective, using instead local points of view that are not integrated into the classical 'gaze at infinity'. As such, according to Merleau-Ponty, Cézanne's paintings show us the structure of the visual world, in which not all objects are attended to at one time from one point of view; instead our perceived world is structured by a plurality of overlapping perspectives within which different aspects are somehow seen together, as aspects of just one world.

Merleau-Ponty's choice here of Cézanne is characteristic. In *Phenomenology of Perception* he often alludes to Cézanne's work in order to illustrate his account of the way in which the visual world forms itself through our gaze.[21] One might be inclined to object that there is in fact a great deal more variety and complexity in the history of painting: Titian's use of space and colour, for example, does not fit within Merleau-Ponty's classical paradigm, but it is also plainly not of the same kind as Cézanne's. But Merleau-Ponty is just using his comparison from the history of painting to illustrate a philosophical theme; he is not offering it as the key to a general account of the depiction of space within painting. So although the cases he discusses are far from exhaustive, the contrast he draws between Cézanne and classical art is, I think, fair enough for his purposes.

Merleau-Ponty concludes his discussion by introducing the perceptual constancies noted by the Gestalt psychologists, whereby the perceived size or shape of an object takes account of our implicit beliefs about its real size and shape; thus a tilted round plate normally looks round (and not oval), and the apparent dimensions of a person's feet when viewed from below do not match the real perspective that is captured by a photograph in which the feet look absurdly large. Merleau-Ponty connects this with the long-standing puzzle that the moon looks so much larger when it is on the horizon than when it is high in the night sky; somehow its apparent size when viewed on the horizon is affected by this context. Merleau-Ponty suggests that this can be explained by perceptual constancies in the horizontal plane, but this cannot be the whole story. Still his general point is right: the space of the perceived world is not the unique space of a 'disembodied intellect', but, like physical space, has different regions which are structured by our expectations concerning the things which we find in them.

## Lecture 3: Exploring the world of perception: Sensory objects

Merleau-Ponty now turns to the things which fill the space of the perceived world. The view he opposes is one which regards these as substances which we experience in a variety of unconnected ways, and whose intrinsic properties have no essential relation to our experience of them. By contrast Merleau-Ponty holds that our experiences are interconnected and reveal to us real properties of the thing itself, which is much as it appears and not some hidden substance that lies beneath our experience of its appearance.

Merleau-Ponty, following Sartre, brings out the inter-connectedness of our experience of things with the examples of honey and lemon. These are both foods, and it is the familiar experience of eating them which gives rise to the tacit gustatory and tactile expectations that are inher-ent in ordinary visual experience, though it is when these expectations are disappointed, as they are by fake foods (e.g. plastic lemons), that the existence of these expect-ations is brought to our attention. Merleau-Ponty's main point, however, concerns the status of the properties mani-fest in ordinary experience. Because these properties, such as the sticky sweetness of honey, can be understood only in the context of our experience of them, there has been a perennial temptation to regard them as superficial appear-ances, merely 'secondary' qualities which need to be backed up by intrinsic 'primary' qualities of things. This is a view which goes back to the Greek atomists, but was influentially revived by Descartes, Galileo and Locke. Against it, Merleau-Ponty holds that we have no good rea-son to downgrade the manifest properties of things even though their definition includes reference to our experi-ence of them. In one way this is right: appearances can be entirely objective, and for that reason there is reason to regard them as appearances of real, genuine, properties, such as colour, taste and the like. But one can still hold that extrinsic properties of this kind presuppose intrinsic properties which explain why things appear as they do. Merleau-Ponty might regard this as merely a scientific hypothesis; but I suspect that it is rather more deeply embedded than that in our ordinary perceived world, since this includes a 'folk science' whereby we presume that it is possible to make sense of why things happen as they do.

## Lecture 4: Exploring the world of perception: Animal life

In the previous lecture Merleau-Ponty emphasised that the perceived world is a human world, a world of things whose character involves a relationship with the human beings who experience them. In this lecture he addresses an anxiety concerning this thesis: that this emphasis on humans implies that there is no proper place for the experiences of 'animals, children, primitive peoples and madmen'.

Merleau-Ponty here anticipates the attention that is now paid to voices that were for long excluded from official histories and philosophies, though he does not recognise the need to include women in his list, and the category 'primitive people' is not one with which we can now feel comfortable. His claim is going to be that it is a character-istic of 'modern' thought, with its rediscovery of the per-ceived world, that it can accommodate these alien voices better than 'classical' thought did. According to Merleau-Ponty classical thinkers (represented here by Descartes and Voltaire) take it that the only voice worth listening to is that of an adult rational civilised human being (and, we might add, a male one), since it is the only voice that makes sense; the experiences of animals, children, primitive peoples and madmen can be summarily dismissed as nonsense. Descartes symbolised this exclusion of the experience of madness when, at the start of his *Meditations*, he simply dismisses without argument the hypothesis that, for all he can tell, he is mad. But, it is worth adding, other philosophers of the classical period were not so dismissive: Hume deliberately includes in his *Treatise of Human Nature* ironic comparisons between humans and animals – where the joke is on the humans.

What, however, of the ability of modern thought to make space for these alien voices? Merleau-Ponty's main claim is that where classical thought saw a sharp division between sense and nonsense, modern thought sees only a difference of degree, accentuated by recognition of the fact that adult life is prone to illness, prejudice and fantasy. Thus although there is still a hierarchy in Merleau-Ponty's position ('Adult thought, normal or civilized, is better than childish, morbid or barbaric thought'), he allows that there are insights in the alien experiences that classical thought excluded, insights which we can ourselves understand and use when we think of the ways in which our own life has been disturbed by illness, childish fixations and other complexities that psychoanalysis has taught us to acknowledge. In the lecture Merleau-Ponty then turns to a brief discussion of animals and the status of their experience, but before commenting on this it is worth reflecting a little on Merleau-Ponty's discussion so far. The most striking point is his hierarchy, with its valuation of 'adult thought, normal or civilized'; for this contrasts very sharply with the romantic valuation of children (as in Wordsworth), of genius, which is often conceived as a form of madness, and of the 'noble savage'. I find it very odd that Merleau-Ponty does not address this line of thought, which will have been very familiar to his audience from Rousseau; perhaps the barbarisms of the Second World War led him to dismiss it. The other point to make is that in *Phenomenology of Perception* Merleau-Ponty frequently draws on accounts of the disabilities of those with brain damage to develop his account of our preobjective bodily experience of the world.[22] So although he discusses the existential significance of these disabilities, the basic theme of his discussion is one of the continuity between the experience of the disabled and that of the normal, rather than the hierarchy emphasised here.

In the closing pages of this lecture Merleau-Ponty turns (as his title always suggested) to the case of animals. As ever he begins by rejecting the Cartesian conception of them as mere machines; instead, drawing on the work of the Gestalt psychologist Wolfgang Köhler, he briefly sketches the way in which one might try to show how an animal 'gives shape' to its world. Merleau-Ponty had discussed this subject at greater length in *The Structure of Behavior*, and he shows there how his existential phenomenology, with its emphasis on preobjective perception and organised behaviour, can readily accommodate animal experience alongside that of human beings.[23] But he ends his lecture here by noting a different way in which animals play a part in the spectrum of experiences he has been concerned to revive, through the symbolic role that animals often play in childish, primitive, and even religious thought.

## Lecture 5: Man seen from the outside

Merleau-Ponty continues his exploration of the perceived world by turning to our understanding of other people. This was already a theme of the previous lecture; but what he is here concerned to discuss is the way in which we can integrate our understanding of others with our understanding of ourselves. He begins, as ever, with Descartes, who famously held that we understand ourselves best when, in self-conscious reflection, we grasp ourselves as just a stream of consciousness that is only contingently connected to a physical body located in physical space (in reading Merleau-Ponty's discussion of this, it is important to note that the translation here uses the two words 'mind' and 'spirit' to translate the single French word 'esprit' in order to capture the connotations of the French word as it occurs in different contexts in Merleau-Ponty's text). As Merleau-Ponty explains later, he thinks that there is something importantly right about Descartes' conception of ourselves. But first he explains why it is unsatisfactory as it stands.

He begins by discussing our experience of others. The Cartesian position notoriously alienates us from others, since it implies that we can know them only indirectly via their behaviour, which is only a detached, contingent, expression of their thoughts and feelings, and one whose interpretation we can never validate since we have no other way of finding out about the other's thoughts and feelings. As against this alienation from others, which rests on the detachment of their mind from their behaviour, Merleau-Ponty, whose discussion at this point exemplifies the phenomenological appeal to 'lived experience', brings forward our experience of another's anger. In this case, he suggests, we have no temptation to detach the other's anger from their behaviour; their anger is 'here, in this room'. The Cartesian separation of emotion from behaviour radically misconstrues our experience of others in this case. Furthermore, he argues, when I reflect on my own anger, I have to recognise that, contrary to Descartes' account of the matter, it too was bound up with my own body, with my gestures, my speech and my behaviour.

Merleau-Ponty then generalises this last point. He suggests that self-consciousness is always dependent upon our consciousness of others, which is inextricably linked to our experience of their behaviour, especially their speech. In this lecture he just cites child psychologists in support of this claim; in *Phenomenology of Perception* he had invoked Husserl's thesis that 'transcendental subjectivity is inter-subjectivity' and argued in detail that there is no coherent conception of self-consciousness which is not regulated by the consciousness that others have of us.[24] So our self-consciousness is always 'mediated' by a language that we have learnt from others and which is dependent upon their use of it. Hence, although Descartes was right to posit the conception of a self that is detached from physical circumstances, this is a 'critical ideal' which expresses the idea of freedom as detachment, and not a metaphysical truth about human beings.

In the last part of the lecture Merleau-Ponty points to the ethical implications of this new picture of human life. It is one in which we can neither escape personal responsibility by imagining that our dependence upon others determines how we are to act, nor escape this dependence upon others by imagining that our freedom enables us to shape our future inalienably. Instead, and this, for Merleau-Ponty, is the 'modern form of humanism', we have to accept that there is an inescapable 'ambiguity' in human life, whereby we have to accept responsibility for our actions even though the significance of everything we try to do is dependent upon the meaning others give to it. It is here that Merleau-Ponty's idiom is recognisably 'existentialist', as he acknowledges the 'anxiety' inherent in this situation and calls for 'courage' in accepting both the inescapability of our responsibility and the impossibility of guaranteeing what our responsibilities will turn out to be.[25] But he disavows the conclusion that human life is therefore inherently absurd, even though it may often appear so. Instead, he urges, we should use humour to prepare 'for those rare and precious moments at which human beings come to recognise, to find, one another'.

## Lecture 6: Art and the world of perception

Merleau-Ponty's aim here is to use the account he has given of the perceived world as the springboard for an aesthetic theory. In doing so he builds on the earlier discussion in Lecture 2 of the way in which modern art (or, at any rate, Cézanne's paintings) helps us to rediscover the creation of the perceived world that we are all too prone to pass over as our attention is drawn to the things that it makes manifest to us. Reciprocally, then, having learnt that the things of the perceived world are manifest to us in experience, and not substances hidden behind a veil of appearances, he wants us to see that much the same is true of works of art. Their meaning is what is given in our experience of them; it does not reside in their relationship to something else, something not perceived but represented.

While it is easy to see how this applies to abstract painting, it is less clear how it applies to representational paintings, such as portraits; for a portrait is clearly intended to be a portrait of someone (Cézanne, perhaps). Yet the portrait is not, as Merleau-Ponty puts it, simply intended to evoke the person portrayed; that would be better achieved by a biography. Instead, the portrait has to be 'a spectacle which is sufficient unto itself', something which cannot be appreciated without seeing it, and which, in the seeing of it, enables us to see the person portrayed in the painting. The meaning must be accomplished within the painting itself, and cannot depend upon a relationship to something extrinsic to the painting, even the person portrayed.

Merleau-Ponty now extends this aesthetic approach to other art forms. Interestingly, he looks forward to applying it to film, and his remarks here are suggestive of the features we do indeed look for in the films we value. In the case of music it is almost too easy to apply his approach, since music is not representational. But the difficulty in this case lies in knowing how to add to formal descriptions of music, for example how to characterise the expressive aspects of music, and Merleau-Ponty does not really contribute to this. In the case of literature, Merleau-Ponty's approach is problematic for the opposite reason. Our appreciation of literature seems to depend on our understanding of the language used, and thus on our grasp of the and created works of art whose meaning is unequivocal, the modern theorist accepts that we are inescapably fallible, and that we should not hope for final solutions in physics any more than in politics. We must learn to live with contestable theories and principles that are inherently provisional; and, equally, be content with works of art that leave open the possibility for a variety of interpretations. It is no good looking for some better conception of reason (e.g. discursive reason) that will definitively show us how to live. We must learn to live not only after the death of God, but also without the dream of reason (these are perhaps the same thing).

Merleau-Ponty does not, however, prescribe a conservative reaction to the failure of the classical ideal of reason, in the manner of, say, Hume and Burke. Instead he affirms the existential ambiguity ('tension' might be a better word) of human life, whereby there is no escape from the requirement to justify our actions, but, equally, no escape from the fact that as we locate our justifications in a space of reasons whose dimensions are set by others, we have to accept that they are bound to be found wanting in some ways. This very affirmation, however, he proclaims to be not just a 'modern truth', but 'a truth of all time', a truth which captures the human condition as it is. As such, he suggests, it should be possible for us to do things which are genuinely worth doing even if they are not informed by the classical ideal; by internalising the ambiguity of human life we should be able to create something as 'solid and lasting' as the paintings of Cézanne.

It is an attractive conclusion. But one cannot help thinking, in a post-modern way, that Merleau-Ponty betrays himself here. If he had really internalised the fallibilism and provisionality of modern thought from which he starts, he should not have allowed himself to present, at the end, his existentialism as a truth that is 'a truth of all time'. A fallibilist does not undermine his fallibilism by taking a fallibilist attitude to it; for fallibilism is inconsistent with dogmatism, not confidence. So we see Merleau-Ponty, at the end of these lectures, poised to move beyond 'modern' thought to postmodernism – but not quite taking the step. But to say this is not to say that these lectures do not present, in the incomplete and sketchy way of modern art, a sketch of a philosophy whose value is 'solid and lasting'.

*The World of Perception*

# 1

# THE WORLD OF PERCEPTION
# AND THE WORLD OF SCIENCE

The world of perception, or in other words the world which is revealed to us by our senses and in everyday life, seems at first sight to be the one we know best of all. For we need neither to measure nor to calculate in order to gain access to this world and it would seem that we can fathom it simply by opening our eyes and getting on with our lives. Yet this is a delusion. In these lectures, I hope to show that the world of perception is, to a great extent, unknown territory as long as we remain in the practical or utilitarian attitude. I shall suggest that much time and effort, as well as culture, have been needed in order to lay this world bare and that one of the great achievements of modern art and philosophy (that is, the art and philosophy of the last fifty to seventy years) has been to allow us to rediscover the world in which we live, yet which we are always prone to forget.

This temptation is particularly strong in France. It is characteristic not just of French philosophy but also of what is rather loosely termed the French cast of mind to hold science and knowledge in such high esteem that all our lived experience of the world seems by contrast to be of little value. If I want to know what light is, surely I should ask a physicist; is it not he who can tell me what light really is? Is light, as was once thought, a stream of burning projectiles, or, as others have argued, vibrations in the ether? Or is it, as a more recent theory maintains, a phenomenon that can be classed alongside other forms of electromagnetic radiation? What good would it do to consult our senses on this matter? Why should we linger over what our perception tells us about colours, reflections and the objects which bear such properties? For it seems that these are almost certainly no more than appearances: only the methodical investigations of a scientist – his measurements and experiments – can set us free from the delusions of our senses and allow us to gain access to things as they really are. Surely the advancement of knowledge has consisted precisely in our forgetting what our senses tell us when we consult them naïvely. Surely there is no place for such data in a picture of the world as it really is, except insofar as they indicate peculiarities of our human make-up, ones which physiology will, one day, take account of, just as it has already managed to explain the illusions of long- and short-sightedness. The real world is not this world of light and colour; it is not the fleshy spectacle which passes before my eyes. It consists, rather, of the waves and particles which science tells us lie behind these sensory illusions.

Descartes went as far as to say that simply by scrutinising sensory objects and without referring to the results of scientific investigations, I am able to discover that my senses deceive me and I learn accordingly to trust only my intellect.[1] I claim to see a piece of wax. Yet what exactly is this wax? It is by no means its colour, white, nor, if it has retained this, its floral scent, nor its softness to my touch, nor indeed the dull thud which it makes when I drop it. Not one of these properties is constitutive of the wax because it can lose them all without ceasing to exist, for example if I melt it, whereupon it changes into a colourless liquid which has no discernible scent and which is no longer resistant to my touch. Yet I maintain that this is still the same wax. So how should this claim be understood? What persists through this change of state is simply a piece of matter which has no properties, or, at most, a certain capacity to occupy space and take on different shapes, without either the particular space filled or the shape adopted being in any way predetermined. This then is the real and unchanging essence of the wax. It will be clear that the true nature of the wax is not revealed to my senses alone, for they only ever present me with objects of particular sizes and shapes. So I cannot see the wax as it really is with my own eyes; the reality of the wax can only be conceived in the intellect. When I assume I am seeing the wax, all I am really doing is thinking back from the properties which appear before my senses to the wax in its naked reality, the wax which, though it lacks properties in itself, is nonetheless the source of all the properties which manifest themselves to me. Thus for Descartes – and this idea has long held sway in the French philosophical tradition – perception is no more than the confused beginnings of scientific knowledge. The relationship between perception and scientific knowledge is one of appearance to reality. It befits our human dignity to entrust ourselves to the intellect, which alone can reveal to us the reality of the world.

When I said, a moment ago, that modern art and philosophy have rehabilitated perception and the world as we perceive it, I did not, of course, mean to imply that they deny the value of science, either as a means of technological advancement, or insofar as it offers an object lesson in precision and truth. If we wish to learn how to prove something, to conduct a thorough investigation or to be critical of ourselves and our preconceptions, it remains appropriate, now as then, that we turn to science. It was a good thing that we once expected science to provide all the answers at a time when it had still to come into being. The question which modern philosophy asks in relation to science is not intended either to contest its right to exist or to close off any particular avenue to its inquiries. Rather, the question is whether science does, or ever could, present us with a picture of the world which is complete, self-sufficient and somehow closed in upon itself, such that there could no longer be any meaningful questions outside this picture. It is not a matter of denying or limiting the extent of scientific knowledge, but rather of establishing whether it is entitled to deny or rule out as illusory all forms of inquiry that do not start out from measurements and comparisons and, by connecting particular causes with particular consequences, end up with laws such as those of classical physics. This question is asked not out of hostility to science. Far from it: in fact, it is science itself – particularly in its most recent developments – which forces us to ask this question and which encourages us to answer in the negative.

Since the end of the nineteenth century, scientists have got used to the idea that their laws and theories do not provide a perfect image of Nature but must rather be considered ever simpler schematic representations of natural events, destined to be honed by increasingly minute investigations; or, in other words, these laws and theories constitute knowledge by approximation. Science subjects the data of our experience to a form of analysis that we can never expect will be completed since there are no intrinsic limits to the process of observation: we could always envisage that it might be more thorough or more exact than it is at any given moment. The mission of science is to undertake an interminable elucidation of the concrete or sensible, from which it follows that the concrete or sensible can no longer be viewed, as in the classical paradigm, as a mere appearance destined to be surpassed by scientific thought. The data of perception and, more generally, the events which comprise the history of the world, cannot be deduced from a certain number of laws which supposedly make up the unchanging face of the universe. On the contrary, it is the scientific law that is an approximate expression of the physical event and which allows this event to retain its opacity. The scientist of today, unlike his predecessor working within the classical paradigm, no longer cherishes the illusion that he is penetrating to the heart of things, to the object as it is in itself. The physics of relativity confirms that absolute and final objectivity is a mere dream by showing how each particular observation is strictly linked to the location of the observer and cannot be abstracted from this particular situation; it also rejects the notion of an absolute observer. We can no longer flatter ourselves with the idea that, in science, the exercise of a pure and unsituated intellect can allow us to gain access to an object free of all human traces, just as God would see it. This does not make the need for scientific research any less pressing; in fact, the only thing under attack is the dogmatism of a science that thinks itself capable of absolute and complete knowledge. We are simply doing justice to each of the variety of elements in human experience and, in particular, to sensory perception.

While science and the philosophy of science have, as we have seen, been preparing the ground for an exploration of the world as we perceive it, painting, poetry and philosophy have forged ahead boldly by presenting us with a very new and characteristically contemporary vision of objects, space, animals and even of human beings seen from the outside, just as they appear in our perceptual field. In forthcoming lectures I shall describe some of what we have learned in the course of these investigations.

simplest of ideas and to revise classical concepts in the light of our experience. Today I would like to consider, as an example of this approach, an idea which seems at first sight to be the clearest of all: the concept of space. Classical science is based on a clear distinction between space and the physical world. Thus space is the uniform medium in which things are arranged in three dimensions and in which they remain the same regardless of the position they occupy. In many cases, the properties of an object are seen to change when the object is moved. If an object is moved from the pole to the equator, its weight and perhaps even its shape will change, on account of the rise in temperature. Yet neither of these changes – of weight and shape – can be attributed to the movement as such: space is the same at the pole as at the equator. The variation which occurs from one place to the other is one of physical conditions, of temperature. Thus the fields of geometry and physics remain entirely distinct: the form and content of the world do not mix. The geometrical properties of the object would remain the same after the move, were it not for the variation in physical conditions to which it is also subject. Or so it was assumed in classical science. Everything changes if, with the advent of so-called non-Euclidean geometry, we come to think of space itself as curved and use this to explain how things can change simply by being moved. Thus space is composed of a variety of different regions and dimensions, which can no longer be thought of as interchangeable and which effect certain changes in the bodies which move around within them. Instead of a world in which the distinction between identity and change is clearly defined, with each being attributed to a different principle, we have a world in which objects cannot be considered to be entirely self-identical, one in which it seems as though form and content are mixed, the boundary between them blurred. Such a world lacks the rigid framework once provided by the uniform space of Euclid. We can no longer draw an absolute distinction between space and the things which occupy it, nor indeed between the pure idea of space and the concrete spectacle it presents to our senses.

It is intriguing that the findings of science should coincide with those of modern painting. Classical doctrine distinguishes between outline and colour: the artist draws the spatial pattern of the object before filling it with colour. Cézanne, by contrast, remarked that 'as soon as you paint you draw', by which he meant that neither in the world as we perceive it nor in the picture which is an expression of that world can we distinguish absolutely between, on the one hand, the outline or shape of the object and, on the other, the point where colours end or fade, that play of colour which must necessarily encompass all that there is: the object's shape, its particular colour, its physiognomy and its relation to neighbouring objects.[2] Cézanne strives to give birth to the outline and shape of objects in the same way that nature does when we look at them: through the arrangement of colours. This is why, when he paints an apple and renders its coloured texture with unfailing patience, it ends up swelling and bursting free from the confines of well-behaved draughtsmanship.

In this drive to rediscover the world as we apprehend it in lived experience, all the precautions of classical art fall by the wayside. According to classical doctrine, painting is based on perspective. This means that when a painter is confronted by, for example, a landscape, he chooses to depict on his canvas an entirely conventional representation of what he sees. He sees the tree nearby, then he directs his gaze further into the distance, to the road, before finally looking to the horizon; the apparent dimensions of the other objects change each time he stares at a different point. On the canvas, he arranges things such that what he represents is no more than a compromise between these various different visual impressions: he strives to find a common denominator to all these perceptions by rendering each object not with the size, colours and aspect it presents when the painter fixes it in his gaze but rather with the conventional size and aspect that it would present in a gaze directed at a particular vanishing point on the horizon, a point in relation to which the landscape is then arranged along lines running from the painter to the horizon. Landscapes painted in this way have a peaceful look, an air of respectful decency, which comes of their being held beneath a gaze fixed at infinity. They remain at a distance and do not involve the viewer. They are polite company: the gaze passes without hindrance over a landscape which offers no resistance to this supremely easy movement. But this is not how the world appears when we encounter it in perception. When our gaze travels over what lies before us, at every moment we are forced to adopt a certain point of view and these successive snapshots of any given area of the landscape cannot be superimposed one upon the other. It is only by interrupting the normal process of seeing that the painter succeeds in mastering this series of visual impressions and extracting a single, unchanging, landscape from them: often he will close one eye and measure the apparent size of a particular detail with his pencil, thereby altering it. By subjecting all such details to this analytical vision, he fashions on the canvas a representation of the landscape which does not correspond to any of the free visual impressions. This controls the movement of their unfolding yet also kills their trembling life. If many painters since Cézanne have refused to follow the law of geometrical perspective, this is because they have sought to recapture and reproduce before our very eyes the birth of the landscape. They have been reluctant to settle for an analytical overview and have striven to recapture the feel of perceptual experience itself. Thus different areas of their paintings are seen from different points of view. The lazy viewer will see 'errors of perspective' here, while those who look closely will get the feel of a world in which no two objects are seen simultaneously, a world in which regions of space are separated by the time it takes to move our gaze from one to the other, a world in which being is not given but rather emerges over time.

Thus space is no longer a medium of simultaneous objects capable of being apprehended by an absolute observer who is equally close to them all, a medium without point of view, without body and without spatial position – in sum, the medium of pure intellect. As Jean Paulhan remarked recently, the space of modern painting is 'space which the heart feels', space in which we too are located, space which is close to us and with which we are organically connected.[3] Paulhan added:

it may well be that in an age devoted to technical measurement and, as it were, consumed by quantity, the cubist painter is quietly celebrating – in a space attuned more to the heart than the intellect – the marriage and reconciliation of man with the world.[4]

In the footsteps of science and painting, philosophy and, above all, psychology seem to have woken up to the fact that our relationship to space is not that of a pure disembodied subject to a distant object but rather that of a being which dwells in space relating to its natural habitat. This helps us to understand the famous optical illusion noted by Malebranche: when the moon is still on the horizon, it appears to be much larger than at its zenith.[5] Malebranche assumed that human perception, by some process of reasoning, overestimates the size of the planet. If we look at it through a cardboard tube or the cover of a matchbox, the illusion disappears; so it is caused by the fact that, when the moon first appears, we glimpse it above the fields, walls and trees. This vast array of intervening objects makes us aware of being at so great a distance, from which we conclude that, in order to look as big as it does, notwithstanding this distance, the moon must indeed be very large. On this account, the perceiving subject is akin to the scientist who deliberates, assesses and concludes and the size we perceive is in fact the size we judge. This is not how most of today's psychologists understand the illusion of the moon on the horizon. Systematic experimentation has allowed them to discover that it is generally true of our field of vision that the apparent size of objects on the horizontal plane is remarkably constant, whereas they very quickly get smaller on the vertical plane. This is most likely to be because, for us as beings who walk upon the earth, the horizontal plane is where our most important movements and activities take place. Thus what Malebranche attributed to the activity of a pure intellect, psychologists of this school put down to a natural property of our perceptual field, that of embodied beings who are forced to move about upon the surface of the earth. In psychology as in geometry, the notion of a single unified space entirely open to a disembodied intellect has been replaced by the idea of a space which consists of different regions and has certain privileged directions; these are closely related to our distinctive bodily features and our situation as beings thrown into the world. Here, for the first time, we come across the idea that rather than a mind *and* a body, man is a mind *with* a body, a being who can only get to the truth of things because its body is, as it were, embedded in those things. We shall see in the next lecture that this is not only true of space but, more generally, of all external objects: we can only gain access to them through our body. Clothed in human qualities, they too are a combination of mind and body.

The unity of the object will remain a mystery for as long as we think of its various qualities (its colour and taste, for example) as just so many data belonging to the entirely distinct worlds of sight, smell, touch and so on. Yet modern psychology, following Goethe's lead, has observed that, rather than being absolutely separate, each of these qualities has an affective meaning which establishes a correspondence between it and the qualities associated with the other senses. For example, anyone who has had to choose carpets for a flat will know that a particular mood emanates from each colour, making it sad or happy, depressing or fortifying. Because the same is true of sounds and tactile data, it may be said that each colour is the equivalent of a particular sound or temperature. This is why some blind people manage to picture a colour when it is described, by way of an analogy with, for example, a sound. Provided that we restore a particular quality to its place in human experience, the place which gives it a certain emotional meaning, we can begin to understand its relationship to other qualities which have nothing in common with it. Indeed our experience contains numerous qualities that would be almost devoid of meaning if considered separately from the reactions they provoke in our bodies. This is the case with the quality of being honeyed. Honey is a slow-moving liquid; while it undoubtedly has a certain consistency and allows itself to be grasped, it soon creeps slyly from the fingers and returns to where it started from. It comes apart as soon as it has been given a particular shape and, what is more, it reverses the roles by grasping the hands of whoever would take hold of it. The living, exploring, hand which thought it could master this thing instead discovers that it is embroiled in a sticky external object. Sartre, who must take the credit for this elegant analysis, writes:

> in one sense it is like the supreme docility of the possessed, the fidelity of a dog who *gives himself* even when one does not want him any longer, and in another sense there is underneath this docility a surreptitious appropriation of the possessor by the possessed.[1]

So the quality of being honeyed – and this is why this epithet can be used to symbolise an entire pattern of human behaviour – can only be understood in the light of the dialogue between me as an embodied subject and the external object which bears this quality. The only definition of this quality is a human definition.

Viewed in this way, every quality is related to qualities associated with other senses. Honey is sugary. Yet sugariness in the realm of taste, 'an indelible softness that lingers in the mouth for an indefinite duration, that survives swallowing', constitutes the same sticky presence as honey in the realm of touch.[2] To say that honey is viscous is another way of saying that it is sugary: it is to describe a particular relationship between us and the object or to indicate that we are moved or compelled to treat it in a certain way, or that it has a particular way of seducing, attracting or fascinating the free subject who stands before us. Honey is a particular way the world has of acting on me and my body. And this is why its various attributes do not simply stand side by side but are identical insofar as they all reveal the same way of being or behaving on the part of the

honey. The unity of the object does not lie behind its qualities, but is reaffirmed by each one of them: each of its
qualities is the whole. Cézanne said that you should be able
to paint the smell of trees.[3] In a similar vein, Sartre writes
in *Being and Nothingness* that each attribute 'reveals the being'
of the object:

> The lemon is extended throughout its qualities, and each
> of its qualities is extended throughout each of the others.
> It is the sourness of the lemon which is yellow, it is the
> yellow of the lemon which is sour. We eat the color of a
> cake, and the taste of this cake, and the taste of this cake
> is the instrument which reveals its shape and its color to
> what may be called the alimentary intuition. . . . The fluid-
> ity, the tepidity, the bluish color, the undulating restless-
> ness of the water in a pool are given at one stroke, each
> quality through the others.[4]

The things of the world are not simply neutral *objects*
which stand before us for our contemplation. Each one of
them symbolises or recalls a particular way of behaving,
provoking in us reactions which are either favourable or
unfavourable. This is why people's tastes, character, and the
attitude they adopt to the world and to particular things
can be deciphered from the objects with which they
choose to surround themselves, their preferences for certain colours or the places where they like to go for walks.
Claudel claims that the Chinese build rock gardens in
which everything is entirely bare and dry.[5] This mineralisa-
tion of their surroundings must be interpreted as a rejec-
tion of the damp of life, as though expressing a preference

for death. The objects which haunt our dreams are meaningful in the same way. Our relationship with things is not a distant one: each speaks to our body and to the way we live. They are clothed in human characteristics (whether docile, soft, hostile or resistant) and conversely they dwell within us as emblems of forms of life we either love or hate. Humanity is invested in the things of the world and these are invested in it. To use the language of psychoanalysis, things are complexes. This is what Cézanne meant when he spoke of the particular 'halo' of things which it is the task of painting to capture.

This is also the message of the contemporary poet Francis Ponge, whose work I shall now offer by way of example. In a study devoted to him, Sartre wrote that,

> Things lived in him for many years. They populated him, they carpeted the furthest recesses of his memory. They were present within him . . . and what he is trying to do now is much more to pluck these monstrous slithering flowers from his inner depths and *render* them than to fix their qualities on the basis of minute observations.[6]

And indeed the essence of water, for example, and of all the elements lies less in their observable properties than in what they say to us. This is what Ponge says of water:

> Water is colourless and glistening, formless and cool, passive and determined in its single vice: gravity. With exceptional means at its disposal to gratify the vice: circumvention, perforation, infiltration, erosion.
>
> The vice plays an inner role as well: water endlessly

---

ravels in upon itself, constantly refuses to assume any form, tends only to self-humiliation, prostrating itself, all but a corpse, like the monks of some orders. [. . .]

You might almost say that water is insane, given this obsession, this fixation, the hysterical need to obey its gravity alone. [. . .]

By definition, LIQUID is what seeks to obey gravity rather than maintain its form, forgoes all form to obey its gravity. And loses all bearing because of this fixation, these unhealthy qualms. [. . .]

Water's anxiety: sensitive to the slightest change of incline. Leaping downstairs two steps at a time. Playful, childishly obedient, returning the moment we call it back by tilting the slope this way.[7]

The same sort of analysis, extended to take in all the elements, is to be found in the series of works by Gaston Bachelard on air, water, fire and earth.[8] He shows how each element is home to a certain kind of individual of a particular kind, how it constitutes the dominant theme in their dreams and forms the privileged medium of the imagination which lends direction to their life; he shows how it is the sacrament of nature which gives them strength and happiness. These studies have all grown out of the surrealist experiment which, as early as thirty years ago, sought in the objects around us and above all in the found objects to which, on occasions, we become uniquely attached, what André Breton called the 'catalysts of desire': the place where human desire manifests itself, or 'crystallises'.[9]

So it is fairly widely recognised that the relationship between human beings and things is no longer one of distance and mastery such as that which obtained between the sovereign mind and the piece of wax in Descartes' famous description. Rather, the relationship is less clear-cut: vertiginous proximity prevents us both from apprehending ourselves as a pure intellect separate from things and from defining things as pure objects lacking in all human attributes. We shall have occasion to return to this point when, in conclusion, we try to establish how our view of the place of human beings in the world has changed over the course of these lectures.

# 4

## EXPLORING THE WORLD OF PERCEPTION: ANIMAL LIFE

In the first three lectures, we argued with respect to science, painting and philosophy that the transition from classical to modern was marked by what might be thought of as a reawakening of the world of perception. We are once more learning to see the world around us, the same world which we had turned away from in the conviction that our senses had nothing worthwhile to tell us, sure as we were that only strictly objective knowledge was worth holding onto. We are rediscovering our interest in the space in which we are situated. Though we see it only from a limited perspective – our perspective – this space is nevertheless where we reside and we relate to it through our bodies. We are rediscovering in every object a certain style of being that makes it a mirror of human modes of behaviour. So the way we relate to the things of the world is no longer as a pure intellect trying to master an object or space that stands before it. Rather, this relationship is an ambiguous one, between beings who are both embodied and limited and an enigmatic world of which we catch a glimpse (indeed which we haunt incessantly) but only ever from points of view that hide as much as they reveal, a world in which every object displays the human face it acquires in a human gaze.

Yet we are not alone in this transfigured world. In fact, this world is not just open to other human beings but also to animals, children, primitive peoples and madmen who dwell in it after their own fashion; they too coexist in this world. Today we shall see that the rediscovery of the world of perception allows us to find greater meaning and interest in these extreme or aberrant forms of life and consciousness. So much so that the whole spectacle that is the world and human life itself takes on new meaning as a result.

It is well known that classical thought has little time for animals, children, primitive people and madmen. You will recall that Descartes saw animals as no more than collections of wheels, levers and springs[1] – in effect, as machines. Those classical thinkers who did not view animals as machines saw them instead as prototypes of human beings: many entomologists were all too keen to project onto animals the principal characteristics of human existence. For many years, our knowledge of children and the sick was held back, kept at a rudimentary stage, by the same assumptions: the questions which the doctor or researcher asked of them were the questions of an adult or a healthy person. Little attempt was made to understand the way that they themselves lived; instead, the emphasis fell on trying to measure how far their efforts fell short of what the average adult or healthy person was capable of accomplishing. As for primitive people, they were either looked to for a model of a more attractive form of civilisation, or else, as in Voltaire's *Essay on Morals*, their customs and beliefs were seen as no more than a series of inexplicable absurdities.[2] Which all goes to suggest that classical thought was caught in a dilemma: either the being that stands before us may be likened to a human being, in which case it can be given, by analogy, the usual human attributes of the healthy adult. Alternatively, it is no more than a blind mechanism – living chaos – in which case meaning cannot possibly be ascribed to its behaviour.

But why were so many classical authors indifferent to animals, children, madmen and primitive peoples? Because they believed that there is such a thing as a *fully-formed man* whose vocation it is to be 'lord and master' of nature, as Descartes put it.[3] Such a man can accordingly, in principle, see through to the very being of things and establish a sovereign knowledge; he can decipher the meaning of every phenomenon (not just those of nature in its physical aspect but also those of human society and history) and explain them by reference to their causes. Ultimately, such a man can locate the particular bodily flaw in the child, primitive, madman or animal, that accounts for the abnormalities which keep them from the truth. For classical thinkers, this is a question of divine law: for they either see human reason as a reflection of the creator's reason, or, even if they have entirely turned their back on theology, they are not alone in continuing to assume that there is an underlying harmony between human reason and the essence of things. From this standpoint, the abnormalities mentioned above can at best be accorded the status of psychological curiosities and consigned condescendingly to a quiet corner of 'normal' sociology and psychology.

Yet it is precisely this conviction, or rather this dogmatic assumption, that science and philosophy of a more mature kind have called into question. In the case of children, primitive people, the sick, or more so still, animals, the world which they occupy – insofar as we can reconstruct it from the way they behave – is certainly not a coherent system. By contrast, that of the healthy, civilised, adult human being strives for such coherence. Yet the crucial point here is that he does not *attain* this coherence: it remains an idea, or limit, which he never actually manages to reach. It follows that the 'normal' person must remain open to these abnormalities of which he is never entirely exempt himself; he must take the trouble to understand them. He is invited to look at himself without indulgence, to rediscover within himself the whole host of fantasies, dreams, patterns of magical behaviour and obscure phenomena which remain all-powerful in shaping both his private and public life and his relationships with other people. These leave his knowledge of the natural world riddled with gaps, which is how poetry creeps in. Adult thought, normal and civilised, is better than childish, morbid or barbaric thought, but only on one condition. It must not masquerade as divine law, but rather should measure itself more honestly, against the darkness and difficulty of human life and without losing sight of the irrational roots of this life. Finally, reason must acknowledge that its world is also unfinished and should not pretend to have overcome that which it has managed simply to conceal. It should not view as beyond challenge the one form of civilisation and knowledge which it is its highest duty to contest.

It is in this spirit that modern art and philosophy have come to reexamine, with renewed interest, those forms of existence which are the most distant from our own. For they bring to light the movement by which all living things, ourselves included, endeavour to give shape to a world that has not been preordained to accommodate our attempts to think it and act upon it. Classical rationalism allowed no middle ground between matter and intellect and ranked living beings without intelligence alongside mere machines; it consigned the very notion of life to the category of confused ideas. Psychologists working today, by contrast, have shown us that there is such a thing as a perception of life and they have tried to describe the various forms this takes. Last year, in an engaging work on the perception of movement, Albert Michotte from Louvain demonstrated that, if lines of light move in certain ways on a screen, they evoke in us, without fail, an impression of living movement.[4] If, for example, two parallel vertical lines are moving further apart and one continues on its course while the other changes direction and returns to its starting position, we cannot help but feel we are witnessing a crawling movement, even though the figure before our eyes looks nothing like a caterpillar and could not have recalled the memory of one. In this instance it is the very structure of the movement that may be interpreted as a 'living' movement. At every moment, the observed movement of the lines appears to be part of the sequence of actions by which one particular being, whose ghost we see on the screen, effects travel through space in furtherance of its own ends. The person watching this 'crawling' will think they see a virtual substance, a sort of fictitious protoplasm, flow from the centre of the 'body' to the mobile extremities which it projects ahead of itself. Thus in spite of what mechanistic biology might suggest, the world we live in is not made up only of things and space: some of these parcels of matter, which we call living beings, proceed to trace in their environment, by the way they act or behave, their very own vision of things. We will only see this if we lend our attention to the spectacle of the animal world, if we are prepared to live alongside the world of animals instead of rashly denying it any kind of interiority.

In experiments conducted as long as twenty years ago, the German psychologist Köhler tried to sketch the structure of the chimpanzee's universe.[5] He rightly observed that the originality of the animal world will remain hidden to us for as long as we continue (as in many classical experiments) to set it tasks that are not its own. The behaviour of a dog may well seem absurd and mechanical if we set it the task of opening a lock or working a lever. Yet this does not mean that if we consider the animal as it lives spontaneously and confronts the questions which lie before it, we will not find that it treats its surroundings in a manner consistent with the laws of a sort of naïve physics and grasps certain relationships to exploit them in pursuit of its own particular goals and, finally, that it works upon its environmental influences in a way that is characteristic of its species.

Centred on the animal is what might be called a process of 'giving shape' to the world; the animal, moreover, has a particular pattern of behaviour. Because it proceeds unsteadily, by trial and error, and has at best a meagre capacity to accumulate knowledge, it displays very clearly the struggle involved in existing in a world into which it has been thrown, a world to which it has no key. In so doing, it reminds us, above all, of our failures and our limitations. It is for all these reasons that the life of animals plays such an important role in the dreams of primitive peoples, as indeed it does in the secret reveries of our inner life. Freud has shown that the animal mythology of primitive peoples is reborn in young children of every generation, that the child pictures itself, its parents and the conflicts it has with them in the animals it encounters. Thus in the dreams of Little Hans, the horse comes to embody as unchallengeable a malefic power as the animals sacred to primitive peoples.[6] In his study of Lautréamont, Bachelard observes that there are 185 animal names in the 247 pages of the *Chants de Maldoror*.[7] Even a poet such as Claudel, who as a Christian might be tempted to under-estimate all that is not human, draws inspiration from the Book of Job and exhorts us to 'ask the animals':

There is a Japanese engraving which shows an Elephant surrounded by blind men. They have been sent as a dele-gation to identify this monumental intrusion into our human affairs. The first of them has put his arms round one of the feet and declares, 'It's a tree'. 'True', says the second, who has found the ears, 'and here are the leaves'. 'Absolutely not', says the third, who is running his hand down the animal's side, 'it's a wall'. The fourth, who has grabbed hold of the tail, cries, 'It's a piece of string'. 'It's a pipe', retorts the fifth, who has hold of the trunk. . . .

The same is true of our Holy Mother Church, which shares the weight, gait and carefree disposition of this sacred animal, not to mention the two-fold protection of pure ivory which protrudes from its mouth. I see the Church with its four legs planted in the waters that descend straight from paradise; with its trunk, it draws them up to deliver a copious baptism along the entire length of its enormous body.[8]

How amusing to think of Descartes or Malebranche reading this passage and finding that the animals which they saw as mechanisms have become trusted bearers of the emblems of the human and the superhuman. Yet, as we shall see in the next lecture, this rehabilitation of the animal world requires a sardonic form of humanism and a particular kind of humour which lay well beyond their reach.

obscurity and confusion. Whereas most people understand spirit to be something like very subtle matter, or smoke, or breath (consistent, in this regard, with primitive peoples), Descartes showed admirably that spirit is something altogether different. He demonstrated that its nature is quite other, for smoke and breath are, in their way, things – even if very subtle ones – whereas spirit is not a thing at all, does not occupy space, is not spread over a certain extension as all things are, but on the contrary is entirely compact and indivisible – a being – the essence of which is none other than to commune with, collect and know itself. This gave rise to the concepts of pure spirit and pure matter, or things. Yet it is clear that I can only find and, so to speak, touch this absolutely pure spirit in myself. Other human beings are never pure spirit for me: I only know them through their glances, their gestures, their speech – in other words, through their bodies. Of course *another human being* is certainly more than simply a body to me: rather, this other is a body animated by all manner of intentions, the origin of numerous actions and words. These I remember and they go to make up my sketch of their moral character. Yet I cannot detach someone from their silhouette, the tone of their voice and its accent. If I see them for even a moment, I can reconnect with them instantaneously and far more thoroughly than if I were to go through a list of everything I know about them from experience or hearsay. Another person, for us, is a spirit which haunts a body and we seem to see a whole host of possibilities contained within this body when it appears before us; the body is the very presence of these possibilities. So the process of looking at human beings from the outside – that is, at other people – leads us to reassess a number of distinctions which once seemed to hold good such as that between mind and body.

Let us see what becomes of this distinction by examining a particular case. Imagine that I am in the presence of someone who, for one reason or another, is extremely annoyed with me. My interlocutor gets angry and I notice that he is expressing his anger by speaking aggressively, by gesticulating and shouting. But where is this anger? People will say that it is in the mind of my interlocutor. What this means is not entirely clear. For I could not imagine the malice and cruelty which I discern in my opponent's looks separated from his gestures, speech and body. None of this takes place in some otherworldly realm, in some shrine located beyond the body of the angry man. It really is here, in this room and in this part of the room, that the anger breaks forth. It is in the space between him and me that it unfolds. I would accept that the sense in which the place of my opponent's anger is on his face is not the same as that in which, in a moment, tears may come streaming from his eyes or a grimace may harden on his mouth. Yet anger inhabits him and it blossoms on the surface of his pale or purple cheeks, his blood-shot eyes and wheezing voice . . . And if, for one moment, I step out of my own viewpoint as an external observer of this anger and try to remember what it is like for me when I am angry, I am forced to admit that it is no different. When I reflect on my own anger, I do not come across any element that might be separated or, so to speak, unstuck, from my own body. When I recall being angry at Paul, it does not strike me that this anger was in my mind or among my thoughts but rather, that it lay entirely between me who was doing the shouting and that odious Paul who just sat there calmly and listened with an ironic air. My anger is nothing less than an attempt to destroy Paul, one which will remain verbal if I am a pacifist and even courteous, if I am polite. The location of my anger, however, is in the space we both share – in which we exchange arguments instead of blows – and not in me. It is only afterwards, when I reflect on what anger is and remark that it involves a certain (negative) evaluation of another person, that I come to the following conclusion. Anger is, after all, a thought; to be angry is to think that the other person is odious and this thought, like all others, cannot – as Descartes has shown – reside in any piece of matter and therefore must belong to the mind. I may very well think in such terms but as soon as I turn back to the real experience of anger, which was the spur to my reflections, I am forced to acknowledge that this anger does not lie beyond my body, directing it from without, but rather that in some inexplicable sense it is bound up with my body.

There is something of everything in Descartes, as in the work of all great philosophers. And so it is that he who draws an absolute distinction between mind and body also manages to say that the soul is not simply like the pilot of a ship, the commander-in-chief of the body, but rather that it is very closely united to the body, so much so that it suffers with it, as is clear to me when I say that I have toothache.[1]

Yet this union of mind and body can barely be spoken of, according to Descartes; it can only be experienced in everyday life. As far as Descartes is concerned, whatever the facts of the matter may be – and even if we live what he himself calls a true *mélange* of mind and body – this does not take away my right to distinguish absolutely between parts that are united in my experience. I can still posit, by rights, an absolute distinction between mind and body which is denied by the fact of their union. I can still define man without reference to the immediate structure of his being and as he appears to himself in reflection: as thought which is somehow strangely joined to a bodily apparatus without either the mechanics of the body or the transparency of thought being compromised by their being mixed together in this way. It could be said that even Descartes' most faithful disciples have always asked themselves exactly how it is that our reflection, which concerns the human being as given, can free itself from the conditions to which it appears to have been subject at the outset.

When they address this issue, today's psychologists emphasise the fact that we do not start out in life immersed in our own self-consciousness (or even in that of things) but rather from the experience of other people. I never become aware of my own existence until I have already made contact with others; my reflection always brings me back to myself, yet for all that it owes much to my contacts with other people. An infant of a few months is already very good at differentiating between goodwill, anger and fear on the face of another person, at a stage when he could not have learned the physical signs of these emotions by examining his own body. This is because the body of the other and its various movements appear to the infant to have been invested from the outset with an emotional significance; this is because the infant learns to know mind as visible behaviour just as much as in familiarity with its own mind. The adult himself will discover in his own life what his culture, education, books and tradition have taught him to find there. The contact I make with myself is always mediated by a particular culture, or at least by a language that we have received from without and which guides us in our self-knowledge. So while ultimately the notion of a pure self, the mind, devoid of instruments and history, may well be useful as a critical ideal to set in opposition to the notion of a mere influx of ideas from the surrounding environment, such a self only develops into a free agent by way of the instrument of language and by taking part in the life of the world.

This leaves us with a very different view of the human being and humanity from the one with which we began. Humanity is not an aggregate of individuals, a community of thinkers, each of whom is guaranteed from the outset to be able to reach agreement with the others because all participate in the same thinking essence. Nor, of course, is it a single Being in which the multiplicity of individuals are dissolved and into which these individuals are destined to be reabsorbed. As a matter of principle, humanity is precarious: each person can only believe what he recognises to be true internally and, at the same time, nobody thinks or makes up his mind without already being caught up in certain relationships with others, which leads him to opt for a particular set of opinions. Everyone is alone and yet nobody can do without other people, not just because they are useful (which is not in dispute here) but also when it comes to happiness. There is no way of living with others which takes away the burden of being myself, which allows me to not have an opinion; there is no 'inner' life that is not a first attempt to relate to another person. In this ambiguous position, which has been forced on us because we have a body and a history (both personally and collectively), we can never know complete rest. We are continually obliged to work on our differences, to explain things we have said that have not been properly understood, to reveal what is hidden within us and to perceive other people. Reason does not lie behind us, nor is that where the meeting of minds takes place: rather, both stand before us waiting to be inherited. Yet we are no more able to reach them definitively than we are to give up on them.

It is understandable that our species, charged as it is with a task that will never and can never be completed, and at which it has not necessarily been called to succeed, even in relative terms, should find this situation both cause for anxiety and a spur to courage. In fact, these are one and the same thing. For anxiety is vigilance, it is the will to judge, to know what one is doing and what there is on offer. If there is no such thing as benign fate, then neither is there such a thing as its malign opposite. Courage consists in being reliant on oneself and others to the extent that, irrespective of differences in physical and social circumstance, all manifest in their behaviour and their relationships that very same spark which makes us recognise them, which makes us crave their assent or their criticism, the spark which means we share a common fate. It is simply that this modern form of humanism has lost the dogmatic tone of earlier centuries. We should no longer pride ourselves on being a community of pure spirits; let us look instead at the real relationships between people in our a vision of things themselves. Reciprocally, a philosophy of perception which aspires to learn to see the world once more, as if in an exchange of services rendered, will restore painting and the arts in general to their rightful place, will allow them to recover their dignity and will incline us to accept them in their purity.

What then have we learned from our examination of the world of perception? We have discovered that it is impossible, in this world, to separate things from their way of appearing. Of course, when I give a dictionary definition of a table – a horizontal flat surface supported by three or four legs, which can be used for eating off, reading a book on, and so forth – I may feel that I have got, as it were, to the essence of the table; I withdraw my interest from all the accidental properties which may accompany that essence, such as the shape of the feet, the style of the moulding and so on. In this example, however, I am not perceiving but rather defining. By contrast, when I perceive a table, I do not withdraw my interest from the particular way it has of performing its function as a table: how is the top supported, for this is different with every table? What interests me is the unique movement from the feet to the table top with which it resists gravity; this is what makes each table different from the next. No detail is insignificant: the grain, the shape of the feet, the colour and age of the wood, as well as the scratches or graffiti which show that age. The meaning, 'table', will only interest me insofar as it arises out of all the 'details' which embody its present mode of being. If I accept the tutelage of perception, I find I am ready to understand the work of art. For it too is a totality of flesh in which meaning is not free, so to speak, but who commission portraits often want them to be good likenesses, but this is because their vanity is greater than their love of painting). It would take us too long to investigate here why, under the circumstances, painters in general tend not to fabricate the kind of non-existent poetic objects that some have produced on occasion. Suffice it to say that even when painters are working with real objects, their aim is never to evoke the object itself, but to create on the canvas a spectacle which is sufficient unto itself. The distinction which is often made between the subject of the painting and the manner of the painter is untenable because, as far as aesthetic experience is concerned, the subject consists entirely in the manner in which the grape, pipe or pouch of tobacco is constituted by the painter on the canvas. Does this mean that, in art, form alone matters and not what is said? Not in the slightest. I mean that form and content – what is said and the way in which it is said – cannot exist separately from one another. Indeed I am doing no more than taking note of an obvious truth: if I can get a sufficiently clear idea of an object or tool that I have never seen from a description of its function, at least in general terms, by contrast, no analysis – however good – can give me even the vaguest idea of a painting I have never seen in any form. So in the presence of a painting, it is not a question of my making ever more references to the subject, to the historical event (if there is one) which gave rise to the painting. Rather, as in the perception of things themselves, it is a matter of contemplating, of perceiving the painting by way of the silent signals which come at me from its every part, which emanate from the traces of paint set down on the canvas, until such time as all, in the absence of reason and discourse, come to form a tightly structured arrangement in which one has the distinct feeling that nothing is arbitrary, even if one is unable to give a rational explanation of this.

Cinema has yet to provide us with many films that are works of art from start to finish: its infatuation with stars, the sensationalism of the zoom, the twists and turns of plot and the intrusion of pretty pictures and witty dialogue, are all tempting pitfalls for films which chase success and, in so doing, eschew properly cinematic means of expression. While these reasons do explain why, hitherto, there have scarcely been any films that are entirely filmic, we can nevertheless get a glimpse of how such a work would look. We shall see that, like all works of art, such a film would also be something that one would perceive. Beauty, when it manifests itself in cinematography, lies not in the story itself, which could quite easily be recounted in prose and still less in the ideas which this story may evoke; nor indeed does it lie in the tics, mannerisms and devices that serve to identify a director, for their influence is no more decisive than that of a writer's favourite words. What matters is the selection of episodes to be represented and, in each one, the choice of shots that will be featured in the film, the length of time allotted to these elements, the order in which they are to be presented, the sound or words with which they are or are not to be accompanied. Taken together, all these factors contribute to form a particular overall cinematographical rhythm. When cinema has become a longer-established facet of our experience, we will be able to devise a sort of logic, grammar, or stylistics, of the cinema which will tell us – on the basis of our

---

knowledge of existing works – the precise weight to accord
to each element in a typical structural grouping, in order
that it can take its place there harmoniously. But as is the
case with all such rule-books where art is concerned, it
could only ever serve to make explicit the relationships
which already exist in successful completed works and to
inspire other reasonable attempts. So the creators of the
future, just like those of today, will still have to discover
new relationships without being guided to them; then, as
now, the viewer will experience the unity and necessity of
the temporal progression in a work of beauty without ever
forming a clear idea of it. Then, as now, this viewer will be
left not with a store of recipes but a radiant image, a particular rhythm. Then, as now, the way we experience works
of cinema will be through perception.

Music offers too straightforward an example and, for
this reason, we shall not dwell on it for long here. It is
quite clearly impossible in this case to make out that the
work of art refers to anything other than itself; program-
matic music, which describes a storm or even an occasion
of sadness, is the exception. Here we are unquestionably
in the presence of an art form that does not speak. And
yet a piece of music comes very close to being no more
than a medley of sound sensations: from among these
sounds we discern the appearance of a phrase and, as
phrase follows phrase, a whole and, finally, as Proust put
it, a world. This world exists in the universe of possible
music, whether in the district of Debussy or the kingdom
of Bach. All I have to do here is listen without soul-
searching, ignoring my memories and feelings and indeed
the composer of the work, to listen just as perception looks

at the things themselves without bringing my dreams into the picture.

Finally, something similar may be said of literature, even though the analogy has often been disputed because literature uses words which also serve to designate natural objects. Many years have already elapsed since Mallarmé made a distinction between the poetic use of language and everyday chatter.[3] The chatterer only names things sufficiently to point them out quickly, to indicate 'what he is talking about'. The poet, by contrast, according to Mallarmé, replaces the usual way of referring to things, which presents them as 'well known', with a mode of expression that describes the essential structure of the thing and accordingly forces us to enter into that thing. To speak of the world poetically is almost to remain silent, if speech is understood in everyday terms, and Mallarmé wrote notoriously little. Yet in the little he left us, we at least find the most acute sense of a poetry which is carried entirely by language and which refers neither directly to the world as such, nor to prosaic truth, nor to reason. This is consequently poetry as a creation of language, one which cannot be fully translated into ideas. It is because poetry's first function, as Henri Bremond[4] and Paul Valéry[5] would later remark, is not to designate ideas, to signify, that Mallarmé and subsequently Valéry[6] always refused either to endorse or reject prosaic commentaries on their poems. In the poem, as in the perceived object, form cannot be separated from content; what is being presented cannot be separated from the way in which it presents itself to the gaze. And some of today's authors, such as Maurice Blanchot,[7] have been asking themselves whether what Mallarmé said

75

of poetry should not be extended to the novel and literature in general: a successful novel would thus consist not of a succession of ideas or theses but would have the same kind of existence as an object of the senses or a thing in motion, which must be perceived in its temporal progression by embracing its particular rhythm and which leaves in the memory not a set of ideas but rather the emblem and the monogram of those ideas.

If these observations are correct and if we have succeeded in showing that a work of art is something we perceive, the philosophy of perception is thereby freed at a stroke from certain misunderstandings that might be held against it as objections. The world of perception consists not just of all natural objects but also of paintings, pieces of music, books and all that the Germans call the 'world of culture'. Far from having narrowed our horizons by immersing ourselves in the world of perception, far from being limited to water and stone, we have rediscovered a way of looking at works of art, language and culture, which respects their autonomy and their original richness.

kind of knowledge and art that is characterised by difficulty and reserve, one full of restrictions. In modernity, we have a representation of the world which excludes neither fissures nor lacunae, a form of action which is unsure of itself, or, at any rate, no longer blithely assumes it can obtain universal assent.

We must indeed acknowledge that, in the modern world (and I have already apologised once and for all for the degree of vagueness which this sort of expression entails), we lack the dogmatism and self-assurance of the classical world-view, whether in art, knowledge or action. Modern thought displays the dual characteristics of being unfinished and ambiguous: this allows us, should we be so inclined, to speak of decline and decadence. We think of all scientific work as provisional and approximate, whereas Descartes believed he could deduce, once and for all time, the laws governing the collision of bodies from the divine attributes.[1] Museums are full of works to which it seems that nothing could be added, whereas our painters display works to the public which sometimes seem to be no more than preparatory sketches. And these are the very works that get subjected to interminable analysis because their meaning is not univocal. Look at the number of studies of Rimbaud's silence after publishing the one and only book that he personally was to offer to his contemporaries. By contrast, how few problems seem to arise from Racine's silence after Phèdre! It seems as though today's artists seek to add to the enigmas which already surround them, to send yet more sparks flying. Even in the case of an author such as Proust, who in many respects is as clear as his classical predecessors, the world he describes for us is neither complete nor univocal. In *Andromaque*, we know that Hermione loves Pyrrhus and, at the very moment when she sends Oreste to kill him, no member of the audience is left in any doubt: the ambiguity of love and hate, which makes the lover prefer to lose the one she loves rather than leave him to another, is not fundamental. For it is quite clear that, if Pyrrhus were to turn his attentions from Andromaque to Hermione, she would be all sweetness and light and fall at his feet. By contrast, who can say whether the narrator of Proust's work really loves Albertine?[2] He observes that he only wants to be close to her when she is moving away from him and concludes from this that he does not love her. Then once she has disappeared, when he hears of her death and is faced with the certainty of a departure with no hope of return, he thinks that he both needed and loved her.[3] But the reader continues to wonder whether, if Albertine were restored to him, as he sometimes dreams is the case, Proust's narrator would still love her? Must we conclude that love is this jealous need, or that there is never love but only jealousy and the feeling of being excluded? These questions do not arise from some probing analysis; it is Proust himself who raises them. As far as he is concerned, they are constitutive of this thing called love. So the modern heart is intermittent and does not even succeed in knowing itself. In modernity, it is not only works of art that are unfinished: the world they express is like a work which lacks a conclusion. There is no knowing, moreover, whether a conclusion will ever be added. Where human beings are concerned, rather than merely nature, the unfinished quality to knowledge, which is born of the complexity of its objects, is redoubled by a principle of it is true that a form of socialism which did not seek support from beyond French national borders would be impossible and, therefore, would lack human meaning. We truly are in what Hegel called a diplomatic situation, or in other words a situation in which words have (at least) two different meanings and things do not allow themselves to be named by a single word.

Yet if ambiguity and incompletion are indeed written into the very fabric of our collective existence rather than just the works of intellectuals, then to seek the restoration of reason (in the sense in which one speaks of restoration in the context of the regime of 1815), would be a derisory response. We can and must analyse the ambiguities of our time and strive to plot a course through them which we can follow truthfully and in all conscience. But we know too much about the rationalism of our fathers to simply readopt it wholesale. We know, for example, that liberal regimes should not be taken at their word, that they may well have equality and fraternity as their motto without this being reflected in their actions; we know that noble ideologies can sometimes be convenient excuses. Moreover, we know that in order to create equality, it is not enough merely to transfer ownership of the means of production to the state. Thus neither our examination of socialism nor our analysis of liberalism can be free of reservations and limitations and we shall remain in this precarious position for as long as the course of events and human consciousness continue to offer no possibility of moving beyond these two ambiguous systems. To decide the matter from on high by opting for one of the two, on the pretext that reason can get to the bottom of things, would be to show that we care less about reason as it operates – reason in action – than the spectre of a reason which hides its confusion under a peremptory tone. To love reason as Julien Benda does – to crave the eternal when we are beginning to know ever more about the reality of our time, to want the clearest concept when the thing itself is ambiguous – this is to prefer the word 'reason' to the exercise of reason. To restore is never to reestablish; it is to mask.

There is more. We have to wonder whether the image of the classical world with which we are often presented is any more than a legend. Was that world also acquainted with the lack of completion and the ambiguity in which we live? Was it merely content to refuse official recognition to their existence? If so, then far from being evidence of decline, would not the uncertainty of our culture rather be the most acute and honest awareness of something that has always been true and accordingly something we have gained? When we are told that the classical work is a finished one, we should remind ourselves that Leonardo da Vinci and many others left unfinished works, that Balzac thought there was, in fact, no way of saying when a work of art has reached the fabled point of maturity: he even went as far as to admit that the artist's labours, which could always continue, are only ever interrupted in order to leave the work with a little clarity. We should also remind ourselves that Cézanne, who thought of his entire oeuvre as an approximation of what he had been looking for, nevertheless leaves us, on more than one occasion, with a feeling of completion or perfection. Perhaps our feeling that some paintings possess an unsurpassable plenitude is a retrospective illusion: the work is at too great a distance from us, is too different from us to enable us to take hold of it once more and pursue it. Perhaps the painter responsible saw it as merely a first attempt or indeed as a failure. I spoke a moment ago of the ambiguities inherent in our political situation as if no past political situation, when in the present, ever bore the traces of contradiction, or enigma, which might make it comparable with our own. Consider, for example, the French Revolution and even the Russian Revolution in its 'classical' phase, until the death of Lenin. If this is true, then 'modern' consciousness has not discovered a modern truth but rather a truth of all time which is simply more visible – supremely acute – in today's world. This greater clarity of vision and this more complete experience of contestation are not the products of a humanity that is debasing itself but rather of a human race which no longer lives, as it did for a long time, on a few archipelagos and promontories. Human life confronts itself from one side of the globe to the other and speaks to itself in its entirety through books and culture. In the short term, the loss in quality is evident, yet this cannot be remedied by restoring the narrow humanism of the classical period. The truth of the matter is that the problem we face is how, in our time and with our own experience, to do what was done in the classical period, just as the problem facing Cézanne was, as he put it, how 'to make out of Impressionism something solid and lasting like the art of the museums'.[4]

# Notes

## FOREWORD

1     Merleau-Ponty's term throughout for these talks is *causeries*, which connotes a communication serious in subject-matter but less formal in tone than a lecture. (Translator's note)

## INTRODUCTION

1     *Phénoménologie de la perception* (Paris: Gallimard, 1945); translated by Colin Smith as *Phenomenology of Perception* (London: Routledge, 1962). Page references are to the new 2002 edition of this English translation.

2     Sartre's account of his childhood is set out in his autobiographical sketch *Les Mots* (Paris: Gallimard, 1964; trans. I. Clephane, *Words*, Harmondsworth: Penguin, 1967). Camus tells his very different story in his posthumously published incomplete novel *Le Premier Homme* (Paris: Gallimard, 1994; trans. D. Hapgood, *The First Man*, London: Penguin, 1996).

---

3   *Phenomenology of Perception* p. 403

4   *La Structure du comportement* (Paris: Presses Universitaires de France, 1942); translated by Alden Fisher as *The Structure of Behavior* (Boston MA: Beacon, 1963).

5   I discuss it at greater length in my introduction to *Maurice Merleau-Ponty: Basic Writings* (London: Routledge, 2003). For a more extended discussion, see *The Philosophy of Merleau-Ponty* by E. Matthews (Chesham: Acumen, 2002).

6   See A. Cohen-Solal *Sartre: A Life* (London: Heinemann, 1987) pp. 164ff.

7   *L'Etre et le néant* (Paris: Gallimard, 1943); translated by Hazel Barnes as *Being and Nothingness* (London: Methuen, 1958).

8   See especially the essay 'The war has taken place' (1945) in *Sense and Non-Sense*.

9   Sartre's long essay about Merleau-Ponty describes their collaboration and eventual parting – 'Merleau-Ponty vivant', *Les Temps Modernes* 17 (1961) pp. 304–76; translated by B. Eisler as 'Merleau-Ponty' in *Situations* (New York: G. Braziller, 1965).

10  *Sens et non-sens* (Paris: Nagel, 1948); translated by H. Dreyfus and P. Dreyfus as *Sense and Non-Sense* (Evanston, ILL: Northwestern University Press, 1964).

11  *Les Aventures de la dialectique* (Paris: Gallimard, 1955); translated by J. Bien as *The Adventures of the Dialectic* (Evanston, ILL: Northwestern University Press, 1973).

12  *Signes* (Paris: Gallimard, 1960); translated by R. McCleary as *Signs* (Evanston: Northwestern University Press, 1964).

13  *Le Visible et l'invisible* (Paris: Gallimard 1964); translated by A. Lingis as *The Visible and the Invisible* (Evanston: Northwestern University Press, 1968).

14  *Phenomenology of Perception* p. 373.

15  *Phenomenology of Perception* p. 458.

16  *Phenomenology of Perception* p. 353.

17  *Phenomenology of Perception* p. 239.

18  *Phenomenology of Perception* p. 241; the reference here to a flaw in the great diamond is to a famous poem by Paul Valéry, *Le Cimetière marin*.

19  *Phenomenology of Perception* p. xv.
20  Although Merleau-Ponty usually takes Descartes to be the paradigm 'classical' theorist, he rightly does not do so here, since Descartes' conception of matter as extension actually resembles Merleau-Ponty's 'modern' conception of space more than the 'classical' conception to which Newton gave the definitive voice.
21  *Phenomenology of Perception* pp. 376–7. Merleau-Ponty also published a fine essay on Cézanne ('Cézanne's Doubt') in *Sense and Non-Sense.*
22  *Phenomenology of Perception* pp. 144–5.
23  *The Structure of Behavior* pp. 93–128.
24  *The Phenomenology of Perception* Part II, Chapter 4 – 'Other Selves and the Human World'.
25  One cannot but be reminded here of Camus' essay 'The Myth of Sisyphus' (in the book of the same title).
26  Elsewhere, when discussing language, Merleau-Ponty places great weight on the 'creative' uses of language; see *Phenomenology of Perception* pp. 207–8.

## 1  THE WORLD OF PERCEPTION AND THE WORLD OF SCIENCE

1  Descartes, *Meditations on First Philosophy*, in *Selected Philosophical Writings*, trans. by Cottingham, Stroothoff & Murdoch (Cambridge: Cambridge University Press, 1988), Second Meditation, p. 80.

## 2  EXPLORING THE WORLD OF PERCEPTION: SPACE

1  Julien Benda, *La France byzantine* ou *Le Triomphe de la littérature pure. Mallarmé, Gide, Valéry, Alain, Giraudoux, Suarès, les surréalistes. Essai d'une psychologie originelle du littérateur* (Paris: Gallimard, 1945).
2  *Joachim Gasquet's Cézanne. A Memoir with Conversations*, trans. by C. Pemberton (London: Thames and Hudson, 1991), p. 221.

3   Paulhan, 'La Peinture moderne ou l'espace sensible au coeur',
    *La Table ronde*, No. 2, February 1948, p. 280. Paulhan uses
    this expression again in a revised version of this article in *La
    Peinture cubiste* (Paris: Gallimard, 1953), p. 174.
4   Paulhan, *La Table ronde*, p. 280.
5   Malebranche, *The Search After Truth*, trans. and ed. by T. Len-
    non and P. Olscamp (Cambridge: Cambridge University Press,
    1997), I, ch. 7, s.5, pp. 35–6.

## 3 EXPLORING THE WORLD OF PERCEPTION: SENSORY OBJECTS

1   Jean-Paul Sartre, *Being and Nothingness. An Essay on Phenom-
    enological Ontology*, trans. by Hazel Barnes (New York:
    Philosophical Library, 1956), p. 609.
2   Ibid., p. 609.
3   *Joachim Gasquet's Cézanne*, p. 151.
4   Sartre, *Being and Nothingness*, p. 186.
5   Paul Claudel, *The East I Know*, trans. by T. Frances and W. Benét
    (New Haven: Yale University Press, 1914).

> Just as a landscape does not consist simply of its grass
> and the colour of its foliage, but is distinguished by its
> outlines and the slope of the ground, so the Chinese liter-
> ally *construct* their gardens with stones. They are sculptors
> instead of painters. Because it is susceptible of elevation
> and depth, of contours and reliefs, through the variety of
> its planes and surfaces, stone seems to them a more
> suitable medium for creating a background for Man than
> are plants, which they reduce to their normal place of
> decoration and ornament. (p. 18)

6   Sartre, 'L'Homme et les Choses', *Situations*, I (Paris: Gallimard,
    1948), p. 227.
7   Francis Ponge, *The Nature of Things*, trans. by Lee Fahnestock
    (New York: Red Dust, 1942), p. 29.

8   Gaston Bachelard, *Air and Dreams* (Dallas Institute of Human-
    ities and Culture, 1988), *Water and Dreams* (Dallas Institute of
    Humanities and Culture, 1999), *The Psychoanalysis of Fire*,
    trans. by Alan Ross (London: Routledge, 1964), *Earth and the
    Reveries of Will* (Dallas Institute of Humanities and Culture,
    2002).

9   Probably an allusion to *Mad Love* (Nebraska: University of
    Nebraska Press, 1987).

## 4  EXPLORING THE WORLD OF PERCEPTION: ANIMAL LIFE

1   Descartes, *Discourse on the Method*, Part Five, in *Selected
    Writings*, p. 45.

2   Voltaire, *Essai sur l'histoire générale et sur les moeurs et l'esprit des
    nations, depuis Charlemagne jusqu'à nos jours* (1753, revised and
    expanded 1761–63).

3   Descartes, *Discourse on the Method*, Part Six, in *Selected
    Writings*, p. 47.

4   Albert Michotte, *The Perception of Causality*, trans. by T. Miles
    and E. Miles (London: Methuen, 1963).

5   Köhler, *The Mentality of Apes*, trans. by E. Winter (London:
    Routledge, 1973).

6   Freud, 'Analysis of a Phobia in a Five-year-old Boy', *Standard
    Edition of the Complete Works of Sigmund Freud*, Vol. X,
    pp. 1–149.

7   Gaston Bachelard, *Lautréamont* (Paris: Corti, 1939).

8   Paul Claudel, 'Interroge les animaux', *Figaro littéraire*, No. 129,
    9 October 1948, p.1. Reprinted in 'Quelques planches du
    Bestiaire spirituel' in *Figures et paraboles*, in *Oeuvres en prose*
    (Paris: Gallimard 'Pléiade', 1965), pp. 982–1000.

## 5  MAN SEEN FROM THE OUTSIDE

1   Descartes, *Discourse on the Method*, Part Five, in *Selected
    Writings*, p. 46:

89

And I showed how it is not sufficient for it to be lodged in the human body like a helmsman in his ship, except perhaps to move its limbs, but that it must be more closely joined and united with the body in order to have, besides this power of movement, feelings and appetites like ours.

See also *Meditations on First Philosophy*, Meditation Six, in *Selected Writings*, p.116: 'Nature also teaches me, by these sensations of pain, hunger, thirst and so on, that I am not merely present in my body as a sailor is present in a ship, but that I am very closely joined and, as it were, intermingled with it, so that I and the body form a unit.'

2  Franz Kafka, 'The Metamorphosis', trans. N. Glatzer, *The Complete Short Stories of Franz Kafka* (London: Minerva, 1992), pp. 89–139.

3  Franz Kafka, 'Investigations of a Dog', *The Complete Short Stories of Franz Kafka*, pp. 278–316.

4  Maurice Blanchot, *The Most High* (Bison Books, 2001).

## 6 ART AND THE WORLD OF PERCEPTION

1  Joachim Gasquet, *Cézanne* (Paris: Bernheim-Jeune, 1926), pp. 130–1.

2  Georges Braque, *Notebooks 1917–1947*, trans. by S. Appelbaum (New York: Dover, 1971), p. 22.

3  Stéphane Mallarmé, *passim*. See, in particular, his *Réponses à des enquêtes* (response to Jules Huret, 1891), in *Oeuvres complètes* (Paris: Gallimard, Pléiade, 1945).

4  Henri Bremond, *La Poésie pure*, his lecture at the public session of the five Academies, 24 October 1925 (Paris: Grasset, 1926).

5  Paul Valéry, *passim*. See, for example, 'Avant-propos' (1920), *Variété* (Paris: Gallimard, 1924); 'Je disais quelquefois à Stéphane Mallarmé ...' (1931), *Variété III* (Paris: Gallimard, 1936); 'Dernière visite à Mallarmé' (1923), *Variété II* (Paris: Gallimard, 1930); 'Propos sur la poésie' (1927), 'Poésie et pensée abstraite' (1939), *Variété V* (Paris: Gallimard, 1944). See

also Frédéric Lefèvre, *Entretiens avec Paul Valéry*, with a Preface by Henri Bremond (Paris: Le Livre, 1926).

6   Paul Valéry, *passim* (in his literary criticism, prefaces, theoretical writings and lectures), for example 'Questions de poésie' (1935), 'Au sujet du *Cimetière marin*' (1933) and 'Commentaires de *Charmes*' (1929), *Variété III* (Paris: Gallimard, 1936); 'Propos sur la poésie' (1927), 'L'homme et la coquille' (1937) and 'Leçon inaugurale du cours de poétique du Collège de France' (1937), *Variété V* (Paris: Gallimard, 1944).

7   See, in particular, *The Blanchot Reader*, ed. by Holland (Oxford: Blackwell, 1995), 'How is Literature Possible?' and Blanchot, *Faux pas* (Paris: Gallimard, 1943), 'La poésie de Mallarmé est-elle obscure?'.

## 7 CLASSICAL WORLD, MODERN WORLD

1   Descartes, *The Principles of Philosophy*, II, Nos. 36–42 in *The Philosophical Writings of Descartes*, trans. by Cottingham, Stroothoff & Murdoch (Cambridge: Cambridge University Press, 1984), Vol. 1.

2   Marcel Proust, *La Prisonnière*, trans. by Carol Clark (London: Penguin/Allen Lane, 2002).

3   Marcel Proust, *Albertine disparue*, trans. by Peter Collier (London: Penguin/Allen Lane, 2002).

4   *Joachim Gasquet's Cézanne*, p. 164.

# INDEX